Library of Congress Cataloging-in-Publication Data is available on file.
Print ISBN: 978-0-692-27034-9

Printed in the United States of America

Your Money Mood

A Woman's Guide to Shift Your Perceptions About Money

By **Susan McEuen,** CFP®, ChFC®

DEDICATION

I'd like to thank all my past and current clients for their inspiration for this book and dedicate it to those women who will bravely take hold of their financial future.

ACKNOWLEDGEMENTS

I'd like to thank Deborah Stroup for providing the encouragement for this book and helping me finally get it to print. The personalities you will find in the book were first developed while Deb and I were sitting on the swing on the front porch of her Bed and Breakfast a few years ago. Julie Glick provided the creative text to my narratives allowing the stories to be told in a fun yet meaningful way. Margo LeChat, my personal trainer, kept my energy and motivation alive to accomplish my dream of this book. Michael Passante, my office partner and dear friend, who provided unwavering belief and additional encouragement. Doug Cristafir of Radiant Arts for helping with the design of my new website and book cover. Last but by no means least, my son Michael and my daughter Megan for being my motivation to see this project to completion. I love and adore you both.

CONTENTS

FORWARD

This is not your typical money book. It is not about cutting up your credit cards, or finding the hottest stock, or showing you how to get rich quick. As you turn page after page you will learn how to make managing your finances less intimidating and much more fun! Imagine having a deep understanding that money is truly your friend.

Most of the women I counsel would prefer to talk about food, exercise, children, relationships, cellulite… anything but money! Why is this? Why do some women abdicate their financial responsibilities while others exert rigid control? And why do some women seem to downright repel money? You probably won't find the real reasons in your conscious mind. Believe it or not, the driving factor behind the financial decisions you make is not necessarily how much you know about money. How would you respond if I were to ask you to close your eyes and answer this question: "How do you feel when you talk about or even just think about spending money, saving money, investing money or not having enough money?" Which emotional responses have just been triggered inside of you? These specific and habitual emotions form what I call your Money Mood.

Chapter 1

<u>Welcome To My Office:</u>

What is it about money, anyway? Few subjects in life are more emotionally charged and anxiety-inducing. Some of us feel completely intimidated by that whole world of stocks and bonds and mutual funds. Some are downright fearful, hoarding our money underneath their mattresses. Others live impetuously in the moment, subscribing to the "spend now, pay later" credo. Some even give it away just to get rid of it. I kid you not! Too many of us live with an unrelenting sense of dread, even shame, around the whole topic of money, especially *our* money.

"A Course in Miracles" defines a miracle as "a shift in perception" and reminds us that miracles are very reasonable to expect. When you shift your perceptions about money, you can literally change the trajectory of your entire life. I've been witness to this time and again in this office of mine, and I would so love to create miracles with you. Your dreams are seeds of the Divine, planted in you for a very specific reason. Only you can do what you came here to do and be who you came here to be. Money need not undermine your every effort, raining stress and struggle on your life's parade. Money can support you, work for you and enable you to live your dreams. This is true, and I can help.

I have been a financial advisor for over 30 years, and I want to invite you into my office. My office is a safe place, a place where you need not feel one ounce of trepidation. In fact, you might just feel as if you're meeting a new friend who has nothing but your best financial interests at heart. Tell me your story and I'll tell you mine. Know that there are no stupid questions. I'll be listening from a place of curiosity and compassion; no judging here. Together we'll figure out how your life has shaped you as a one-of-a-kind individual.

You may have made some decisions that sent you down a path or two you'd rather not have traveled. You may even feel embarrassed to admit some of these mistakes. First of all, join the club! Second, commend yourself on having the courage to take an enormous step toward heading in the right direction. And rest assured that together we can and will change the course of your financial future. By understanding who you uniquely are and what motivates your money decisions, we will create not only solutions, but also a future that excites and inspires you.

Allow me to provide a glimpse into what is possible for you. Let's say you're out to lunch with a friend you haven't seen in a while. You share one of those rare and wonderful friendships that have stood the test of time. No matter how many months or years pass without seeing one another, you always seem to pick up where you left off. Your friend's looking good… It's more than her beautiful features, her figure or her outfit. She's got a distinctive aura about her now. She seems genuinely happy and remarkably stress-free, even in this economy. Go figure.

You discuss everything from kids and family to work and relationships, but not money. You've never been at all inclined to broach that subject. It's very clear that your friend is enjoying her life. She's giving off a powerful, I'm-in-control-of-my-life vibe, and you just have to know why. So you decide to just go for it and ask her what is making her feel so optimistic and self-assured. Your friend tells you that she has a financial advisor she's been working with for the past few years. "I've learned so much from her and for the first time in my life, I feel confident and in control of my financial future. It's *such* a relief…" You find yourself wondering if those words could ever come out of your mouth. "Well, shoot--I want to feel that way too!" you declare. "You two will definitely click," says your friend, as she smiles and gives you my contact information. Taking a deep breath, you make a life-affirming decision and set up an appointment to meet with me.

As you pull into the parking lot in front of my office you begin to feel more than a little apprehension. You've anticipated most of the potential questions I might have for you, or at least you hope you have. And you're nervous about having to admit mistakes you've made in this particularly intimidating world of money. You remind yourself that you're here to remedy this and more as you step out of the elevator and walk through my door.

I greet you with a warm, friendly smile and a professional handshake. We sit down at my conference table as if we're meeting in your kitchen. I reassure you that there is no such thing as a stupid question and that I am here to help you feel more in control of your money. Then we begin to discuss what brought you to my office. We all have our own unique story–a story that shapes who we've become and how we function in the world of money. To make you feel more comfortable, I set the stage by sharing with you my story.

I was raised by a single mother of four in a time when women did not have, nor did they even try to establish, their own financial credit history. My mother lived under the pressure of debt her entire life. No matter how hard she worked, she was always behind in payments, never able to get ahead. Just when it seemed that financial things were finally looking up, something would break down–a dishwasher, an air conditioning unit, a car, and *ahead* became *behind* once again.

There were times, scary times, when there was no food in our house. I remember opening the cabinets and finding them just about empty. My mother had no college education, so she was forced to work several jobs at minimum wage just to try to make ends meet. What pressure she must have felt, all the time. She worked hard and was so proud when she was finally able to afford to buy a house for all of us. But when it came time for the mortgage to be approved, she needed my father's signature. I remember feeling for her then–all that work for all those years and still, she wasn't enough.

I vowed that I would learn everything there is to know about money and savings and establishing credit so I would not find myself in such a precarious, dependent position. The more I learned and the harder I worked, the more I earned and the more money I saved. I established excellent credit and became an expert in money management, from learning how to budget to managing investments and retirement accounts, etc. Once I became financially secure, I knew that it was my mission to teach and motivate others to do the same.

At this point, you're feeling much more comfortable and, I hope, rather inspired. After all, if I can become financially savvy and secure, you can too. You no longer have to climb that mountain of money management alone. We're in this together, you and me.

Next I explain that your finances are like a big jigsaw puzzle. Each piece affects your entire puzzle picture and you're just missing a few. First we will need to look at the various pieces, including your tax return, your income, your expenses, assets and liabilities--the logical, practical pieces of your puzzle.

Just as a physician can use your blood work to make a diagnosis, so too can I utilize the information you provide me with to diagnose your financial health. I can determine what you value by how you spend your money. I can also find ways to save you money when I learn more about how you're spending it. I'll ask you about your family, past and present. How did you learn about money while growing up? Who are you supporting now? Most importantly, I want to learn your Money Mood: the underlying beliefs, emotions, and desires that have been determining your money decisions. Step by step we'll figure out what you've learned about money throughout your life, as well as what *really* makes you want to spend or save, give or invest. More and more pieces of your puzzle are coming together.

I become your motivator, encouraging and coaching you every step of the way. I ask you to share with me your dreams, your hopes for the future. The better you and I can clarify your personal priorities and define your dreams, the better you and I can piece together what you really want out of life--for yourself and the ones you love. What you and I will work on together goes far beyond the math. Which inspires you more: thinking about the number of dollars in your bank account, or picturing the life you want for yourself and your loved ones? Therein lies your *ultimate* motivation. As we piece together more and more of your compelling reasons in just the right places, your stress-reducing and smile-inducing future becomes crystal clear and oh, so inviting.

My job is to educate you about your financial options and to create a plan that not only fits you and your lifestyle, but also will help bring your dreams from "maybe someday..." to actual, factual fruition as well. You absolutely *can* feel more in control of your financial future. Your trusted financial advisor believes in you. We will develop a long-term relationship because we really *are* in this together. All it takes is an openness to learn and your commitment to stay on the path that leads to those desires of your heart.

Are you ready to create miracles? Your dreams are calling...

Chapter 2

<u>What's Your Money Mood?</u>

You may be wondering why I refer to your relationship to money as your "Money Mood." If you were to Google the word *mood*, you'd find several meaningful definitions.

1 - A conscious state of mind or predominant emotion
2 - A receptive state of mind predisposing to action
3 - A distinctive emotional quality or character
4 - A temporary state of mind or feeling

Let's look at these definitions one by one. "A conscious state of mind or predominant emotion." Aha! A *conscious* state of mind, so we're not necessarily on auto-pilot, destined to unconsciously repeat patterns of behavior that stem from predominating emotions, especially when they no longer serve us. Good to know…

"A receptive state of mind predisposing to action." This would imply that we are able, and hopefully willing, to receive something new--to consider suggestions and ideas that just might predispose us to take healthier actions. An open mind is a most wonderful and absolutely necessary attribute on our path to a prosperous life.

"A distinctive emotional quality or character." It's highly likely that most of us have come to distinguish our habitual proclivities when it comes to our relationship with money. We may already define ourselves as more of a spender or a saver. We may have learned to identify ourselves as someone who is an over-giver or a high achiever. And we cling so tenaciously to these identities of ours, whether they serve us or not.

Thankfully, the qualities and characteristics that have previously prevented us from living a financially abundant life are *not* immutable. They can be changed…

"A temporary state of mind or being." Temporary, not etched in stone permanently. We were not born with an incurable deficiency when it comes to managing money. Over time we have acquired certain inclinations and perspectives. We often come to perceive the world and our options in ways that limit and frustrate us to no end. But we can work miracles, remember? We can shift those perceptions from life-limiting to life –affirming. We can change and improve our Money Moods, I promise.

Here's something interesting to ponder: Your relationship with money affects every aspect of your life, and every aspect of your life affects your relationship with money. I have noticed time and again that the ways in which we relate to money often parallel the ways in which we relate to everything from food to relationships and, most significantly, to ourselves. For example, your Money Mood might also reflect your Food Mood. So if you tend to over-indulge in or restrict one, chances are you will also tend to over-indulge in or restrict the other. I have noticed both in my own life and in those of my clients, that there is usually an over-arching theme that weaves its way through our lives. Therefore, insights that you may have already uncovered about your belief systems in one arena of your life may well apply to how you relate to money, too. And as you dig deep and come to understand your Money Mood(s), these illuminating discoveries may shed some healing light on other parts of you and your life. So feel free to draw every possible parallel and connect every definitive dot. The more we learn about ourselves, the more we can heal the parts of ourselves that may have inadvertently steered us off course. Your money miracles can begin with just one AHA! So here we go--let the insights roll!

Chapter 3

<u>Before You Take the Money Mood Quiz...</u>

It's time to create a lot of fun around a topic that is frequently viewed as anything but: money. Talk about a shift in perception… What if learning about your own personal Money Mood could actually be enjoyable? What if this new revelation about you and your relationship to money could actually lighten you up? What if you could find your way to believing that money is your friend? All of this and more is possible.

In every aspect of life, very few things are completely black and white. I don't know about you, but I sometimes feel an internal resistance to being categorized or slotted. Like you, I know that there is so much more to me than this particular aspect or that particular tendency. Throughout almost three decades of advising hundreds of clients, I have found it supremely helpful to really get to know each person I meet so I can individualize my advice and ultimately our financial plan accordingly. Although there are many variations on behavioral themes and attitudes about money, there are four predominant and distinctive characteristics or traits that we will address in this book.

Chances are you will be a hybrid. Very few of us operate from only one Money Mood. When you take this quiz, choose the answers that most accurately reflect how you think and what you do most of the time. You might occasionally find yourself feeling torn between two answers, so I have a suggestion. If you can't decide which fits your relationship with money best, imagine how someone who knows you very well might answer for you. The Money Mood Quiz is designed to contribute to your self-awareness. No self-condemnation allowed. Each Money Mood has its own pros and cons; after all, sometimes your attributes can work to your detriment and vice versa.

By the way, you might just find yourself smiling as you take the quiz. Will wonders never cease? Finding humor in a subject that usually feels so heavy–who knew? In fact, some of the examples of character traits and behaviors are both humorously and deliberately magnified to help clearly distinguish one Money Mood from another. If ever there was a time to take a light-hearted approach to a serious matter, it's now! Remember, you can *always* change your mood. Knowing who you are and how you relate to money is the first step on the way to your prosperous life. So step inside, take the quiz, and have some fun!

MONEY MOOD QUIZ

1 – When I think about saving money for my future:
    A. I believe that the Universe will align everyone and everything necessary to bring my dreams to fruition, so enjoying today is the only way to go! (D)
    B. It feels like I will never accumulate enough financial assets so I'd better buckle down, work harder, and save more 'cause you never know… (F)
    C. I get a little panicky because I always seem to give my money away, which has not left much in the way of savings for me and my future. (G)
    D. I feel pressure hoping I calculated accurately so that I am putting enough money into my IRA, my savings account, and my investments for my children's future. (P)

2 – As far as following a budget goes:
    A. Budget schmudget! What a drag… I prefer to be spontaneous and deal with paying the bills later. (D)
    B. I am proud to say that I am a minimalist. My needs are simple, and I am extremely disciplined when it comes to adhering to my budget. (F)
    C. I closely monitor monthly expenses and stay within a strict budget, but I always feel that I could be more vigilant. (P)
    D. I have to admit that I squeak by most months because I have trouble saying *No* when there are so many worthy causes. (G)

3 – The way I feel about credit cards is:
    A. I don't like 'em. I pay everything with cash, checks, or money orders. (F)
    B. They're a convenient but necessary evil. They make me nervous, so I pay them off in full every month. (P)

C. I try to pay at least the monthly minimums. I tend to buy a lot of gifts with my credit cards. (G)
D. Love 'em! Well, I love them when I'm at the mall, but when it's time to pay bills… not so much. (D)

4 – I would borrow money:
    A. If the loan was short-term with a competitive interest rate. Even then I'd feel anxious about re-paying it ASAP. (P)
    B. To build an animal shelter. (G)
    C. To buy my dream home, take vacations, get a Mercedes Benz. (D)
    D. As a last resort. I never want to owe anything to anyone. (F)

5 – My adorable Uncle Fred unexpectedly left me $75,000 in his will. I am inclined to:
    A. Feel relieved to have so much money to put toward my kids' college fund, but worried that I might not be investing it in the best way. (P)
    B. Have a whopper of a shopping spree followed by that trip to Australia that I've always wanted to take, flying first class, of course! (D)
    C. Put half in my savings account and cleverly hide the other half in my house. (F)
    D. Give to my favorite charities and help out my brother and his family. Then I'll see if there's any money left to pay my bills. (G)

6 – To me money means:
    A. Security. Spending it makes me feel uneasy, but saving it makes me feel proud and safe. (F)
    B. Philanthropy. I do my best to stay on top of my bills, but money is for sharing and giving and making a difference. (G)

C. Pleasure! Spending it gives me such an instant gratification rush. (D)

D. Reward. The harder I work, the more I should be compensated. (P)

7 – If, God forbid, I had to deal with an emergency:

A. I'd be feeling stress-overload for not being as thrifty a saver and as shrewd an investor as I could have been. (P)

B. I'd be freaking out. I guess I would have to rely on the kindness of strangers… (D)

C. I'd be upset with myself for having given away what I should have been saving… (G)

D. I'd scramble around my house and find all of the money I've secretly socked away. (F)

8 – I'm in the mall and I see something I don't really need, but I REALLY want, so:

A. I would feel guilty treating myself to something frivolous when there are so many people and animals suffering in our world. (G)

B. I'm buying it! Carpe diem! It makes me happy to buy what I want, and being happy is the purpose of life! (D)

C. I am not about to blow my money diet! Besides, I'm addicted to *saving* money, not spending it. (F)

D. I'd have to feel that I have worked hard enough to earn a reward to even consider buying something like that. (P)

Note: ANSWER KEY for Money Mood Quiz can be found in the Appendix.

Chapter 4

<u>Introducing the Money Mood Women</u>

You are about to meet the four Money Mood women: Debtor Danielle, Frugal Francesca, Generous Genevieve, and Perfectionist Penelope. These women represent the most predominant Money Moods of the women I have advised in my practice. I recommend reading each and every story. Even if you find that you relate more to Penelope, for example, than you do with the others, chances are that you know (maybe even live with) Danielle, Francesca and/or Genevieve. I also find that many of my clients are hybrids, so to speak.

Here too you may find that the characteristics and behaviors of the four Money Mood women are somewhat exaggerated. I don't know about you, but sometimes I have to be shown in Technicolor what I have not fully recognized in black and white. And yes, I am also hoping to add some levity now and again to this traditionally heavy topic of money.

We will be following Debtor Danielle, Frugal Francesca, Generous Genevieve, and Perfectionist Penelope on their journeys. We begin with "a day in the life" of each woman to understand their individual and habitual thoughts, feelings, and behaviors. By the time each Money Mood woman returns for her follow-up visit, you will see what used to be self-defeating modi operandi have transformed into self-awareness followed up with healthier behaviors. What may seem like baby step after baby step on this path to financial abundance adds up over time to giant leaps in the right direction. Just as in life, the more we focus on the financial journey rather than that far off, some-day destination, the more we enjoy and appreciate the here and now.

Danielle, Francesca, Genevieve, and Penelope are courageous, remarkable women. Just like you. Whoever you are and wherever you've been, know that your financial prosperity is only one or two changed beliefs away.

Chapter 5

<u>Debtor Danielle</u>

Debtor Danielle walks into the mall feeling that familiar anticipatory sense of excitement. She's on a buy-now-pay-later mission. It's Friday, and Danielle has had a particularly rough week as a busy buyer at Spendingdales. Being over-worked and under-appreciated really bites! She still has some room on a credit card or two, doesn't she? Credit cards don't really feel like money anyway. Danielle gets to buy now! She'll deal with that paying part later, but in this moment she needs to feel instant gratification from buying herself that coat, those shoes, these earrings… STAT!

Danielle leaves the mall, swinging her shopping bags, smiling and humming with glee. She feels positively euphoric as she deposits her much-needed designer doodads and adorable adornments in the back seat of her leased BMW and pulls out of the parking lot. Driving home, Danielle feels a sense of self-righteous entitlement surging through her. She deserves to look good and feel good right now! And doesn't the Dalai Lama, or some other wise dude, remind us to live in the moment every chance we get? Immediate pleasure is Danielle's modus operandi so why plan for some far off future? While waiting at a red light, she feels a shiver of anxiety about compulsively over-spending, again. She distracts herself by imagining just how she's going to look in her new mix-and-match accoutrements on her upcoming vacation to Aruba. Aaahhh, that's better. "Saving, schmaving!" Danielle declares. "Spend it while you've got it, I always say!"

Danielle's friends do admire her sense of adventure and her carpe diem ways. But few of them know just how much loss she has experienced in her young life. Danielle has said far too many premature goodbyes. And she's had her sense of security ripped out from under her too many times to count. Danielle knows all too well that the future is promised to no one, so she lives as if there may be no tomorrow. While commendable in some ways, seizing the precious present without considering consequences can be a precarious way to live. In the back of her mind, Danielle is actually aware of this, but at this stage in her life impetuosity still prevails. So she buys what she wants to buy and lives where she wants to live.

On her way to her ocean-front condo, Danielle goes to her mailbox to retrieve a bunch of bills. "Ick… I hate these things. What a buzz kill." Shaking off the uneasy sensation, Danielle gets online to answer emails, check out her Facebook, tweet to her heart's content and generally surf away her worries on the web. It's times like this when her PhDDD in Procrastination and Rationalization really serves her well. And, OMG! She almost forgot to watch the latest episodes of "American Idol" and "Dancing with the Stars!" Danielle runs to her TiVo, turns on her flat screen TV, plunks down on her leather couch with her remote control, and covers herself in a blanket of denial.

After a weekend of lunches and dinners with friends in addition to yoga and Private Pilate's classes, Danielle resigns herself to her Sunday night bill-paying routine. She can be responsible, on occasion. But oy, what a drag. She squeaks out enough from her bank account to cover rent, utilities, and the ever-increasing minimum payments on five of her credit cards. Danielle closes her eyes and rubs her temples when those old, familiar, and extremely unsettling waves of dread begin flow through her. She courageously cracks one eye open as she clicks on the balance of her online checking account. Yikes… consequences really suck. Danielle momentarily ponders taking a second job to pay down her massive credit card debt. In one of her more creatively desperate moments, she finds herself wondering if she could teach a course in Orgasmic Shopping at the local night school. If only she could morph into Barbara Eden, in "I Dream of Jeannie"...

Morphing instead into Scarlett O'Hara, Danielle shrugs her shoulders, grabs a pen, scribbles "Buy lottery ticket!" on a sticky note, attaches it to her front door, and calls one of her fun-time friends. She'll scale that mountain of debt another day.

Chapter 6

<u>Frugal Francesca</u>

Frugal Francesca felt very proud of herself today. Not only did she repair her own formerly flat front tire, she also bought her shampoo, conditioner, toothpaste, deodorant, paper towels, wrapping paper, laundry detergent, cat food… a plethora of necessities (in bulk), all at the dollar store. OK, the paper towels fell apart when they got the slightest bit wet. And as she was folding her freshly washed and dried clothes she did notice some funky film all over them. Then her normally ravenous cats sniffed the new discount cat food, made the strangest faces, and flicked their tails as they walked away in disdain. "Well, you always have to compromise somewhere," Francesca reminded herself. So she has to be extra careful with the paper towels, she'll brush the mysterious fuzz off her clothes somehow, and her finicky felines will eventually want to eat the new food. Well, two outta three ain't bad…

In her defense, Francesca was raised on copious amounts of fear, struggle, and guilt–the fear of her family once again losing their home and possessions, the struggle of never making ends meet, and the guilt on the rare occasion when her family could actually pay their bills but had to bear the resentment of those who still could not. She knew the embarrassment of wearing ill-fitting clothes from the local thrift shop. She was all too familiar with the sense of helplessness and vulnerability associated with going without heat, electricity, and often food. Sometimes Francesca and her family would stay in one home for several years. Just when she'd start to feel safe and secure, her father would once again lose his job (through no fault of his own, of course). Her hopelessly dependent and despondent mom would pack up her family's meager possessions, and young Francesca would find herself living in destitution once more. As they drove away in shame and desperation, Francesca promised herself that when she was a grownup, she would do anything and everything to make sure that she would never ever feel unsafe, unprotected, or unprepared again.

So is it any wonder that Francesca now maintains the tightest of controls over every conceivable aspect of her life? From her vegan diet to her tri-athlete fitness program to the income she earns as an underwriter at McThrifty Insurance Company, she is ruthlessly rigid with herself. Somehow it feels right, or maybe *familiar*, to push herself and to go without. "Needs are necessary, wants are indulgent" she declares. Francesca is proud of the discipline it takes to stick to her rigorous routines and regimens. The key to success is self-control, so she reins in her desires, shops only for her bare necessities, and only makes purchases when they are on sale. Pay full price? You've *got* to be kidding me! Buy something on a whim? I don't think so! Relax and enjoy yourself? Not so much…

To her credit, Francesca has taken control of her life in her own way. She chooses to have no credit cards and no checking account. Even when it's inconvenient, she only pays with cold, hard cash. The whole concept of credit cards has always baffled her. How can you spend what you don't have? Francesca researches and evaluates and takes her time in making every decision. Impetuosity can lead to financial disaster, and she's had enough of *that* in her life, thank you very much!   And those big banks are just out to get you with all of those ridiculous fees, so forget about a checking account. It's much less complicated this way. Francesca really does prefer the simple lifestyle. In fact, she has been president of her local chapter of Minimalists of America for the past six years. She likes counting her money repeatedly and hides her stash in places such as her underwear drawer, a light bulb socket, the freezer, and the ever popular under-the-mattress. You just never know when that treacherous money shoe will drop. Francesca prefers "safe" because she's had far too much "sorry."

Most of the time, Francesca just functions on auto-pilot, living her simple and oh-so predictable life. Although every now and then, she does question whether or not fear is the best motivator. Once in a blue moon she does long for more fun and laughter in her life. And more and more frequently, Francesca wonders how much longer she can hold this beach ball of self-denial under the water.

Chapter 7

<u>Generous Genevieve</u>

Genevieve would not know herself if she didn't have to contend with perpetual money pressures. Managing the thriving Woof and Purr Veterinary Clinic for the past 27 years has actually provided her with what many would consider to be a generous income. She's worked hard, really hard, all her life. Yet when the paychecks come in, Genevieve finds herself unconsciously thinking thoughts like, "Great! Now I can help out my dear friend who is really hurting…" and "Look at that poor little baby from the third world country… those sweet little puppies and kittens… those beautiful dolphins and whales… I just *have* to give generously to help them however I can!" and "My sister really needs an iPod to cheer her up. I'll send her a surprise gift!" While in so many ways Genevieve is a truly selfless person, she actually gets a major rush from giving. In fact, she often feels selfish in her acts of generosity–after all it is *she* who gets the heart rubs.

For years and years Genevieve has constantly used self-talk and gone to therapy to delve deeply into her life experiences. She has concluded that somehow her unconscious mind is like a broken record, spinning erroneous beliefs like "I don't deserve…. Struggling is noble… Money scares the hell out of me… Investing in the stock market or mutual funds, etc. is completely intimidating… People will resent me if I have money and they don't." Such negative associations she has with the money she needs to sustain her. At times she feels as if she has become money-repellent and, in a way, she has. If only Genevieve would finally allow money to flow *to* her instead of pushing it away. Yet she persists in giving and giving, and usually from an empty cup.

Genevieve could start her own support group: Over-Givers Anonymous. "Hi, my name is Genevieve and I am an over-giver." "Hi, Genevieve…" All too often she has trusted those untrustworthy people who have their greedy little self-entitled radar set for altruistic people like her. And oh, how she has been manipulated and taken advantage of by such people… repeatedly. Even with ALL of those painful experiences, Genevieve's default mantra remains "It just feels so good to give!" And yes, it undoubtedly does.

But Genevieve has one major flaw in her thinking. Time and again, she leaves herself out of the giving equation! More often than she cares to admit, Generous Genevieve has forgotten to adequately provide for herself, much less spend her money on something so frivolous as a massage or a vacation. She would feel downright self-indulgent if she got a facial when there are so many hungry children and animals in the world. And the word "NO" is exceptionally hard for her to say. In her more courageous and conscious moments Genevieve *might* say, "I can't give you a yes on that right now…" Maybe Genevieve should travel by airplane more often so she would be reminded of that all important, self-preserving instruction, "Put your own oxygen mask on first!"

After all is said and done, Genevieve is drained–financially, physically and emotionally. She has to work harder and harder to keep up with her live-to-give ways. While others have wisely invested in their financial future, much to her detriment Genevieve has been focused instead on the instant gratification she gets from giving. She is stressed from the pressure of having too much month left at the end of the money. She has no sense of security, either. What if she gets sick (again)? Downsized (again)? Whatever will she do to support herself? And what about her rapidly approaching retirement years? Yeeesh… Genevieve is filled with trepidation and deficient in sleep. Tossing and turning, she often wonders, "Where did I go wrong? Why is it always so hard for me to save money? And where is my bottle of Struggle-Be-Gone?! There has *got* to be a better way!" Yes, Generous Genevieve, there most certainly is…

Chapter 8

Perfectionist Penelope:

Perfectionist Penelope sits at her desk feeling tension course through her veins. Working for Always Striving Surgical Sales Company is inherently stressful. Throw in her everything-to-everybody single-mother tendencies, and her sky-high standards have her internal stress-o-meter boinging off the walls! She closes her eyes as those old familiar "never-good-enough" thoughts flood her mind. She pinches the bridge of her nose as she feels another headache coming on and reminds herself to take a deep breath. Then she smiles as she remembers a funny bumper sticker she saw on a car today that said, "Don't believe everything you think!" "Right," she says out loud. "Gotta remember that one more often... at least 7,000 times each day."

Penelope reviews every piece of her particularly productive, but frequently frustrating, day and automatically seems to focus on what she could have done better. Her alarm clock rang at 4:30am, as usual. And before she was fully conscious, Penelope's t-shirt, shorts and sneakers were donned and she was flying out the door for her four-mile power walk. She was almost one full minute over her usual pace, and although she did cut into sleep to get in a workout one too many times this past week, she wasn't about to let herself off the slacker's hook. She could have done better, and tomorrow she would. Wasn't exercise supposed to de-stressify? Maybe if she joined a gym and had some fun... Nope, nope, nope! What was she thinking? Her daughter starts college in the fall. Does she have enough in the college fund? And her son is still growing like a weed and needs a new wardrobe every other month... Whoops -- times a-wastin'! Penelope regroups, weighing and measuring each ingredient in her morning smoothie. It looks and tastes like something from the swamp but it's making her cells happy, so her mouth will just have to deal with the flavor and glug it on down.

As Penelope showers, applies her make-up, and dresses for her day, the same old self-flagellating thoughts seep from her unconscious to her conscious mind. "Geez, I don't have as much muscular definition as I did when I was a competitive diver…" and, "Oh, hell–not another gray hair!" and "There is not enough cover-up in the world to hide these circles under my eyes." Never mind that she hasn't competed in diving in over three decades, or that her 12 gray hairs are barely even visible to the naked eye, or that those circles under her eyes are from chronic sleep-deprivation. She has let herself down, again. Whenever people compliment Penelope on her fit physique and her beautiful features, she outwardly mumbles "Thank you" while inwardly she thinks, "Oh, ye of low standards…"

One last hyper-critical look in the mirror and Penelope is off to wake the kids. She's got to stay on top of her adorable ADHD 14-year-old son in addition to making sure her "I'm not a morning person" 17-year-old daughter doesn't pour orange juice into her bowl of Cocoa Krispies. When both kids are finally fed, dressed, and ready to go to school, Penelope grabs her thermos full of high-test coffee, rushes out the door, drives the kids to school, and heads to her first appointment.

Penelope was able to get into three surgical suites today. The first one was an operation with a vascular surgeon who she finally persuaded to switch to her product line. The other two were with open-heart surgeons who agreed to trial her auto-transfusion system. Penelope could pat herself on the back for the extensive product knowledge, the tenacity and the sales skills necessary to work with these in-demand, prestigious surgeons. She could acknowledge the years it has taken her to earn the right to teach these surgeons how to use her products in the middle of such complex and critical procedures. She could even commend herself on being in the top 5% of her company's sales force while single-handedly raising two children. Instead, Penelope plagues herself with criticism for a missed opportunity here and a slightly-less-than-perfect presentation there.

As she speed-walks to her car, Penelope finds herself mumbling the same old refrain, "There's just never enough time…" She shifts gears into mom-mode, picks her kids up at school, drops her daughter off at swim team practice, and takes her son to his soccer game. Penelope often finds herself feeling that her body is in one place while her mind is in another. As she watches her son play soccer, she worries about everything she has to get done before she goes to bed: prepare for working with her manager tomorrow, fill out her weekly sales report, pay her bills, etc. Soccer game over, she hugs her son and hustles him out to the car. She picks up her daughter, and they zip back home. By the time she prepares dinner, talks with her kids, and helps them with their homework, its 9:30p.m.

Penelope plunks down at her desk exhausted, but she pushes through to cross every "t" and dot every "i." What if she's not completely prepared? What if each performance isn't better than the last? What if she pushes so hard that she gets sick and can't work to support her family? What if, what if, what if?! It does not occur to Penelope that she could actually ask for help now and then. She only knows that if she doesn't do it, it won't get done. As Penelope feels the internal pressure building and building, she finds herself wondering how much longer she can allow fear to feed her life's momentum. Like a manic hamster on a wheel, she pushes herself on and on, never daring to step off lest she hit that proverbial wall…

Chapter 9

DREAM TIME!

If I had a dime for every time I heard a woman say, "But going for my own dreams is selfish… especially when my kids need so much, in this economy, blah, blah, blah…" Well, I would have a boatload of dimes! I hear you, I applaud your giving heart, and I've been known to think and feel the same way myself. But truth be told, you've stopped short of getting the point(s). I've said it before and I'll say it again (reminding myself all the while) that flight attendants all over the world have the answer! You've got to put your own oxygen mask on before you can do anyone you love any good. Get it? Got it? Good! I'll remind you if you remind me…

Throughout my 30+ years as a financial advisor, I have been witness to many of my clients working so hard for so long, denying their own passion much of the time, all the while focusing on making it to the 65-year-old (or 66 years and 8 months) retirement-age finish line with enough savings to sustain them. I always admire the incredible discipline and dedication needed to reach this destination. I absolutely encourage everyone I advise to be as financially prepared as possible for their golden years. But, all too often I have seen these clients experience overwhelming regret when they cross that elusive finish line only to be too stressed out and exhausted and/or disabled to enjoy this long-awaited reprieve. Or worse, they celebrate their retirement only to pass away from a heart attack or cancer before they make it to their next birthday. Their "Someday I'll…" mantra was just not enough to bring their dreams to fruition. As my client base has aged I have found myself wondering more times than I can count: Did these people whom I have come to really care about ever accomplish what they dreamed of for themselves? Or have they been operating from fear for so long that they have ultimately postponed their dreams right out of existence? Unfortunately, the "I'll suffer and struggle for decades and then I can be happy" method of functioning rarely succeeds.

Nothing would make me happier than to bring my decades of observations and insights to you so that they shine the light on the big picture of your life. When you cross your own proverbial finish line, I want you to experience passion and fulfillment rather than regret and dejection. This just may call for another miracle – another shift in perception. Far too frequently we women feel responsible for everyone else in our lives. Could be in our DNA, could be part of the way we were raised… probably a little of both. Lest we forget, we are all genetically coded to live to our fullest potential! This means that we not only have to take care of ourselves, it also means that we owe it to ourselves (and the world, by the way) to bring those dreams that live within us to fruition.

I've heard it said that a great deal of our existential pain is due in large part to circling our gifts. We dance around what we *really* want to do, what we came here to do. I do realize that these days our lives are overflowing with the have-to's and consequently are almost devoid of the want-to's. I understand the day-to-day stress and strain of living in such a fast-paced, chockful-of-choices society. And I also know that it often takes us twice as long to do half as much because we are running on fumes too much of the time. If ever there was a time to "fill 'er up," it's now.

I whole-heartedly believe that our dreams are seeds planted within us by God, Spirit, the I AM Presence… whatever you choose to call the Divine Source. These dream seeds are one-hundred percent unique to each one of us, and yours can only take root and grow within YOU. I'm going to channel the wisdom of John Lennon now and ask you to *imagine*. Just take a moment and put whatever and whoever is causing you stress in your day to day life into the "I'll get to you later" department. I promise you, making the most of your Dream Time will have a profoundly positive impact in the quality of your life. And it happens to be a mighty enjoyable process to boot!

OK, here we go… Imagine how you'd feel if you bounced out of bed each morning happily anticipating another day of work/play in your ideal career. Imagine earning a prosperous living by turning one of your all-time favorite hobbies into your major source of income. Imagine having enough of a financial cushion to be able to get a weekly massage, or take that vacation to your favorite place on the planet, or learn how to fly a plane like Chuck Yeager, dance like Gene Kelly, or play the cello like Yo-Yo Ma. Imagine having more than enough money to give generously to every charity you've ever wanted to support. Imagine having the financial wherewithal to go back to school to study what has always made your heart sing!

Can't you feel the joy bubbling up inside? Talk about watering those dream seeds of yours. Creating a life based on what you desire most allows you to give from overflow, instead of struggling with constant underflow. So when you come right down to it, it is anything *but* selfish to live a life that enables you to be your best Self.

By looking through the filter of your own dreams, you'll find that you have more than enough incentive to do whatever it takes to create financial security for yourself and the ones you love. It is absolutely essential that you connect your dreams with everything from adhering to your budget to saving for your 401K. Now achieving your financial goals takes on a whole new and compelling meaning. Stay tethered to the dreams for your future that bounce you out of bed, whenever you go shopping, pay your bills, and balance your checkbook. It will transform your entire outlook and fuel your sense of purpose. Overtime you'll find that both you and your bank account will be more than filled up.

Growing Your Dreams:

Stay with me in this space of potential, with your visionary mindset. We'll get back to "reality" (whatever that is…) soon enough. For now, suspend those recurring thoughts that command you to be practical. I promise you, we will weave your dreams in beautifully with that which is actual and factual in your life. It's time to pull your dreams out of the someday-maybe ethers and concretize them into this 3-D world in which we live.

If you need to burn sage, listen to meditation music, and quiet your mind, then "OOOOMMMMM" your way there. If you need to channel your five- or six-year-old Self, do so. If you need to take a big poster board and draw with colored crayons, go for it. If you need to put on your favorite music and dance like no one's watching, have a blast! Do whatever it takes to get in the Dream Time zone of possibilities, OK? OK!

Did you do it? Are you in the Dream Time zone? If not, find your own unique way to get out of the practicalities of your left/logical brain and jump into the wonders of your right/creative brain. We'll wait for you… take your time… find your way… aaaaannd you're there--excellent! Now we can begin.

What did you want to do or be when you "grew up?" A ballerina? President of the United States? The mommy-est mom? A doctor? A musician? All of the above? No limits–just write...

If you miraculously had quadrupled the free time you have now, what would you want to do? How would you spend this gift of time? What would you finally "get around to doing?" Would you throw more parties for your friends and family? Would you take a course in something that really floats your boat? Spend more time with the one(s) you love? Would you volunteer? Learn sign language? Play the piano? Take classes in tap-dance? Hike? Bike? Skate? Meditate? What would be the most fulfilling way(s) you would spend your new-found time? What really lights you up?! Ponder, smile, and write...

If you suddenly had ten times the amount of money your presently have in your bank account, what would you do with it? What would you buy? Where would you go and with whom? How would you spend your days? Would you hire a personal trainer? Make reservations at those "up-scale" restaurants you've always wondered about? Would you go to concerts or plays? Take a cruise? Go back to school to be a (fill in the blank)? Would you move? Where to? What type of home would you love to own? Close your eyes and picture this prosperous life of yours. What sounds do you hear? What smells do you smell? What tastes do you taste? How does living this life of abundance feel inside of you? Open your eyes, tap into your stream of consciousness, and write!

Let's really dig deep and access your heart's desires. It's time to access not only your right/creative mind, but your heart as well. What would you change in your life to be truer to the Soul of you? Your career? Your style of dressing? Who might you let go of... and who might you welcome in? What gifts would you want to give and to whom? What causes would you want to support and why? What contributions do you want to make to your community, your country, our world? Who is your most authentic YOU? What do you want your legacy to be?

Review everything you've written. Add even more, if you like! Now, either highlight or underline anything and everything that really moves you, takes your breath away, and makes you do the happy-hum... OK. Now circle which dreams you must have, be, or experience so that you will feel truly fulfilled in your life. If you've put your all into answering these questions, you will have just uncovered the fruits of your dream seeds...

You did it! Kudos to you! Pat yourself on your back and take a deep breath... I'm very proud of you. It takes courage to bring forth your dreams and put pen to paper. And it takes commitment to bring what you've envisioned into your everyday life. So we need to water these dream seeds, nurture them and help them grow. Here's what we're going to do...

Take a couple of minutes and write down a goal for each of your dreams.

Chapter 10

<u>The Necessity Board</u>

While Danielle, Francesca, Genevieve, and Penelope have distinctly different Money Moods, they all need to give themselves the same essential gift: the truth. In order to create a healthy, wealthy relationship with money, begin by giving yourself the gift of honesty.

In my practice I have worked with hundreds and hundreds of bright, successful, and resourceful people. Yet when it comes time to look at how they are budgeting/spending their money, the strangest things tend to occur. Some people will mysteriously leave out a shopping spree here and a mani-pedi there. Others will include a detailed list of every conceivable monthly expense, but never actually total it all up. A fair amount of my clients master the art of procrastination in the most creative ways. In other words, they avoid looking at what they do not want to face.

If, for example, you wanted to drop some pounds, it would be a good idea to know how much you actually weigh. While this absolutely makes logical sense, our emotions often shift into over-drive to avoid the potential pain of seeing that dreaded number on the scale. Who among us cannot relate to this scenario? But this tactic rarely, if ever, leads to successful weight loss.

I would be remiss in my job as your financial advisor if I advocated denial in any way, shape, or form. And just as with everything else in life, the more integrity and effort you put into every exercise in this book, the more you will ultimately get out of it. Your initial reality check need not be a painful experience for you. I recommend accurately recording all of your expenses and viewing this entire exercise from a place of curiosity. "Will you look at that? I had no idea I spent that much money on coffee or gifts or hair care products each month…"

You might want to think of this as a treasure hunt: a game in which you discover extra money in your own wallet. Every penny found can be used to build your net worth. Every dollar uncovered can be applied to the fruition of your dreams. It all adds up--in surprisingly pain-free ways, I might add. Remember, you and I are in the process of improving your financial situation by evolving your Money Mood consciousness, step by step.

You're going to record only your absolutely-must-pay monthly bills and expenses on your Necessity Board. Your rent or mortgage payment is definitely necessary. But going out to dinner four nights a week? I think we can all agree that this falls under the "optional" category.

Now it's time to introduce *your* Necessity Board! Notice, I did not refer to this as your budget. After thirty plus years as a financial advisor it is crystal clear to me that the word *budget* can elicit a variety of non-productive reactions including all kinds of self-criticism from shame to blame. Throw in truckloads of denial and barrelfuls of juicy justifications, and you'll get a glimpse of what I have been witness to throughout the years.

If you're one of the few who hears the word *budget* and feels proud and excited at the prospect of sharing your money monitoring masterpiece, rest assured that you will feel equally thrilled by recording these expenses on your Necessity Board.

Whether you feel trepidation or elation, it matters not. This is your personal diary of what you absolutely need to financially survive month to month and year to year. So, accurately recording your necessary monthly expenses is what ultimately counts.

This is step one in putting together your financial puzzle picture, so we will need all of your necessary puzzle pieces. Think of these monthly necessities as the pieces that create the borders of your puzzle. Once we determine how much money you have after all of your necessary expenses have been paid, we can begin to fill in more of your puzzle with "the fun stuff." I promise.

Living within your means often requires exercising some restraint, no question about it. The delayed gratification you experience in the short run will lead to a financially secure future which, by the way, is the main ingredient needed to create your peace of mind.

Note: A Necessity Board you can personalize can be found in the Appendix

Chapter 11

<u>The Reward Board</u>

Just as yin needs yang and dark needs light, you need a reward after being so honest with yourself and so diligent in recording your absolutely-must-pay expenses on your Necessity Board. The only financially *and* psychologically sound way to remain motivated enough to stay this course is to reward yourself, even a little every month if money is temporarily tight. The more "extra" money you discover by living within your means, the better you and I can create both instant and delayed (but oh-so-necessary either way) gratification.

Your short-term reward might include a new pair of shoes, a rock-climbing class, some charitable donations, or even a massage. As long as you are rewarding yourself only from the extra money you found after paying for all of your monthly necessities *and* you are doing so in ways that enhance your life, I say go for it! You've earned it, after all.

If you find yourself slipping back into old, self-defeating behavior, don't beat yourself up. First of all, remember that you are a work in progress. Just like changing any habit, it takes practice. Your habits are wired into your brain as actual physical connections. Over time you can create neural pathways that are stronger than the one you wish to change.

The basic secret of using your mind power to change a habit is this: (1) Stir up and allow yourself to truly "feel" intense emotion about what you wish to change; (2) select a new positive behavior or thought pattern; (3) associate your new pattern with even stronger positive emotion; (4) reward yourself with praise each time you replace the old pattern with the new one; and (5) make it a point to repeat this as often as possible.

Does this seem too simple? What you are doing is actually creating physical changes in your brain–rewiring the neural pathways that create the power of the mind. As Dr. Joe Dispenza, author of Breaking the Habit of Being Yourself says: "In the infinite sea of potentials that exist around us, how come we keep recreating the same realities? The brain does not know the difference between what it sees and what it remembers."

Secondly, most people find themselves thinking and acting in ways that have been habituated for many, many years. As they say, you can't whip a u-turn with the Queen Mary. But you can head in a healthier and wealthier direction, little by little. That's what this book is really all about. Making the most of your Money Mood(s) is a step-by-step process. You will find yourself becoming more and more conscious of your thoughts and actions with regard to money. You will begin to replace that which no longer serves you with that which truly does. Before you know it, you have increased your net worth, and then…

Reward Board

(Below are examples of items that
might be on your personal reward board)

Short Term Goals
- ☐ Mani-Pedi every month
- ☐ Hair extensions and color
- ☐ Buying an expensive fashion handbag
- ☐ Day trip of antiquing
- ☐ Trip to wine country
- ☐ Rock climbing class
- ☐ Join a yoga center
- ☐ Build a cash reserve for emergencies
- ☐ Pay down some debt

Longer Term Goals
- ☐ 65 inch smart screen TV with surround system
- ☐ European vacation
- ☐ Trip to Australia
- ☐ Volunteer in a foreign country
- ☐ New $40,000 car
- ☐ New luxury home on a lake
- ☐ Early retirement

Chapter 12

<u>Debtor Danielle Returns</u>

Danielle walks into my office looking slightly sheepish. As she hands me the financial information I requested in our first visit, I notice that Danielle is not really making eye contact with me. The more we discuss her financial situation, the more she avoids looking at me. I need to lighten her up but quickly, so I stop talking mid-sentence and Danielle finally looks up. I say with a warm smile, "Danielle, you're behaving like a dog who's being reprimanded for snatching a piece of food from the table." She squinches up her face and looks at me like I've lost my marbles. "You know how they look down, sideways, anywhere but in your eyes? Why do you think they do that? What do you think they're feeling in that moment?"

Danielle sits back in her chair, talking a deep breath and says, "That dogs feel guilt… and shame for misbehaving."

"And you?" She hangs her head and tells me that she feels a lot like that poor pooch. "Danielle," I respond, "here's what I want you to know. I am not here to scold you. First and foremost, know that my office is a safe place, so never will I ever wag a shaming finger at you. I am here to be your financial educator and motivator. I am your coach, cheering you on as you learn and grow and change the course of your life. We're in this together, remember? I'm on your side." Danielle's mouth turns up at the corners as she looks at me with a combination of relief and hope. "Now, we are *really* ready to begin!"

At this point I explain to Danielle that her "homework" represents the logical and practical pieces of her puzzle.

Gathering all of that information might seem about as exciting as a piece of dry toast, but stay with me–the juicy part's coming! As we review her financial paperwork, more of her puzzle pieces come together for us.

I share with Danielle that my way of relating to my clients involves getting to know their history, their families, their life philosophies… anything that will help me better understand them and their Money Mood. After all, treating the symptom and not the cause heals only temporarily, if at all. Hidden beneath our actions are emotions that motivate us to behave in certain ways. We discuss Danielle's habitual impulsivity when it comes to spending money. She is aware enough to recognize her instant gratification modus operandi and that it does not always work in her favor, particularly with regard to money.

Danielle begins by telling me a little about her upbringing. She has experienced a lot of painful personal losses–from loved ones to her home. Now she realizes that her "live as if there's no tomorrow" outlook goes much deeper than just being spontaneous and in the moment. I explain to Danielle that as a culture, we've gotten too adept at finding ways to go numb. Better to go to the mall than to feel pain or grief, anger or frustration, shame or guilt. Unfortunately, the momentary relief Danielle experiences is inevitably followed by more of the very emotions she was attempting to avoid, once the consequences of her actions come back to bite her in the butt, so to speak.

I can practically see the light bulb turning on within Danielle as she connects dot after dot. "There's your first AHA!" I exclaim. We just uncovered some of the causes beneath her over-spending symptoms. Now she has choices and options, where she once had only her habitual, unconscious, and all too often self-defeating behaviors. Danielle's miracle, her shift in perception, will now serve to heighten her awareness in those just-about-to-spend-money moments. Now she can begin to make healthier, more responsible choices.

Time for solutions! When I start to explain the "pay yourself first" concept, I can see Danielle getting all kinds of excited. "I like this solution!" she exclaims.

 I smile and say, "I hope you feel the same after I make some points of clarification. For example, by making more than your minimum credit card payments each month, you are actually paying yourself first."

Danielle looks positively perplexed. "What the…? I don't get it. I know I need to pay down my credit cards, but how is that paying myself first?"

"Your credit card balances are so high that you're barely paying the interest charges," I explain. "Those exorbitant payments you have to make each month are seriously depleting your bank account. If you want to have more expendable income in your future, you need to pay yourself first by decreasing your credit card debt now. Delayed gratification, I know. But you're heading toward no gratification at all unless you begin making wiser choices today."

"I get it," Danielle reluctantly concedes. "There are no holes in that one," she says, looking a little glum. I can tell she needs some encouragement, so I point out that she is only months away from paying off one of her credit cards. She perks right up. "Really?"

"Yes! I usually recommend paying down your credit cards with the highest interest rates first. I definitely do want you to reduce your balance on those cards. But right now I suggest taking what might feel like a baby step, because I really want you to feel that sense of accomplishment from paying down that credit card as soon as possible."

"I get it," says Danielle. "And I'll do it!"

I remind Danielle of the dream she shared with me in our first meeting. She wants to own a gorgeous six-bedroom home with an indoor pool and plenty of closet space. We discussed beginning with saving for the down-payment on a starter home and then working her way up to her dream mansion. I reassure Danielle that we will work toward saving and investing her money. "In fact, I bet you will eventually become addicted to saving rather than spending money," I confidently state.

"Tall order," says Danielle.

"Not necessarily," I reply. "Let's connect saving money to those dreams of yours. Now what happens to your desire and inclination to save rather than spend?"

I introduce Danielle to the Reward Board and recommend that she consider the following: Perhaps you could consider rewarding yourself with a mani-pedi after you have paid all of the minimum credit card balances for two months in a row.

Then I explain that the better Danielle adheres to paying for necessities, the sooner she will be able to flip her Necessity Board over and find… her Reward Board! She lights up like a Christmas tree as she lists categories including: entertainment, clothing, travel, gym membership, and self-care/pampering. I remind her that she can only spend money on her rewards if there is overflow after she's paid for all of her necessities.

"Putting all of these pieces in place and following this new plan really does allow you to enjoy yourself on the path to financial security," I tell Danielle .

"Go figure!" she says. "I never thought I could look forward to saving more than spending. You're absolutely right–it *is* a miracle!" That's all it takes…

Note: On the next page is the Necessity Board that Danielle completed.

NECESSITY BOARD for Debtor Danielle
(Net Monthly Income = $5103)

Expenses:	$
Rent	$ 1300
Cleaning Lady	$ 100
Utilities	$ 300
Internet, Cable, etc.	$ 195
Groceries	$ 500
Dining	$ 300
Car lease payment	$ 500
Fuel	$ 200
Parking	$ 60
Medical Insurance payment	$ 250
Dental, vision & other expenses	$ 30
Prescriptions	$ 80
Massages	$ 200
Cell Phone	$ 125
Personal Trainer	$ 200
Mani-Pedi/Hair	$ 200
Professional Services, ie, Legal, Accountant	$ 70
Credit Cards (Shopping sprees, etc.)	$ 700
Total	**$ 5310**
Left Over for rewards	**ZERO**

Note: Danielle is actually spending more than she makes each month and putting it on credit cards increasing her debt.

Chapter 13

<u>Welcome Back, Frugal Francesca</u>

I greet Francesca with a firm handshake and a warm smile. "Good to see you again," I say.

"Same here," she replies with a nod and a somewhat stilted grin. She's wearing black slacks with a white button-down shirt and though she's very fit and trim, there is a feeling of heaviness about her. I also notice that she's holding tight to a shopping bag. I recall from our first visit that it took me a little while to loosen Francesca up, so I begin by asking how her cats are doing. "Freddie and Freda are fine," she answers. "As finicky, funny, and frisky as ever..."

I smile. "You're certainly alive with alliteration today, aren't you?" Excellent... An answering smile spreads across her face and I can feel the tension factor in the room decreasing significantly.

"Are you ready to begin?" I ask. "Sure," she says, as we head over to my conference table. Francesca reaches into her shopping bag and pulls out three manila envelopes. One is labeled "Income," the next "Expenses," and the last "Savings." As I read through the contents of each one, Francesca nervously taps her pen on the table. She has calculated every penny earned and spent with astounding accuracy and attention to details. "Your record keeping skills are to be commended," I tell her. "I've never seen anything like it. You are quite possibly my most meticulous client, Francesca!" She looks at me as if she's not sure if I'm actually complimenting her. "I'm very impressed," I clarify. "I wish all my clients were as thorough and honest as you are!"

"Thanks," she says with relief. "I have to… I just have to stay on top of every penny, 'cause you never know."

"You never know?"

"You never know when the rug will get ripped out from under you, so you have to be prepared for the worst case scenario at all times. As an underwriter, I identify and calculate risk every single day. It takes good judgment to make sound decisions. This is my philosophy, and I only feel comfortable when I'm playing it safe."

In our first meeting, Francesca shared some experiences from her childhood with me–it was unstable, to say the least. So, I'm not at all surprised by her financial records, given her world view. "Please share with me how you prepare for these potential dire circumstances," I request.

"First of all, I rely only on myself – no one else."

"Why is that?"

"Because I'm the only person I can trust," says Francesca.

"OK go on."

"Because I don't trust banks, I take care of all of my money," she continues. Francesca notices my perplexed expression and says, "Well, I actually store all of my money, my cash to be precise, in certain locations in my home."

"I see."

"And I do not buy frivolous things, at all. I mow my own lawn, I fix my appliances and I shop for bargains like nobody's business," she says emphatically.

—

"I'm sure you do."

Francesca sits with arms folded, looking more than a little defiant. "The first time we met," I remind her, "you agreed that it's time to have an objective person analyze your financial situation. I truly admire how far you've come and how much you do for yourself, Francesca. But you wouldn't expect your electrician to remove a kidney, would you?"

"Of course not," she replies.

"Your professional expertise is in underwriting and mine is in managing people's money. I like to think that we have mutual respect between us."

"We do," Francesca says. "I wouldn't be here if I didn't respect you."

"I thank you for that. I would appreciate the opportunity to earn your trust as well. And that will take time." She nods in agreement. "The way I see it, the only way I can truly earn your trust is for you to know beyond a shadow of a doubt that I have your best interests at heart."

"Very true," says Francesca.

"I'm confident that over time my words and my actions will reinforce your trust in me. So I'm going to start by challenging some of your beliefs." She looks a little taken aback so I continue. "For example, you said that you store your money in the tangible form of cash in your house."

"I do," she says. "I hide my money in a couple of places, just in case. Makes me feel more secure and in control."

"I hear you. But what happens if, God forbid, there's a fire in your home? Money is made of paper, correct?"

Francesca looks horrified as she slowly nods her head. "I hadn't thought of that," she admits.

"So maybe if you put at least *some* of your money in the bank, it would actually be safer there," I suggest.

"Maybe…" she replies.

"Believe me, Francesca, I'm very happy to hear that you place such a high priority on financial security," I tell her. "Having said that, I'm concerned about your financial future."

"Why is that?"

"Because by not investing your money, you're going broke safely," I explain. "The cash you're hiding in your home could be multiplying exponentially for you. Not only that–the money you're holding onto yourself is actually worth less each year due to inflation. And you don't even have an IRA. I would be remiss if I didn't point out that you actually have a false sense of financial security." I pause, letting Francesca wrap her mind around what I've just said. "What would happen if for some unforeseen reason you were unable to work? What if you experienced a pay cut, or even lost your job?" I ask.

She shudders. "How would you take care of yourself? How would you take care of Freddie and Freda?" She's going into panic mode now, so I quickly reassure her. "Francesca," I say, "don't worry. After all, you're here! You're working with me.

If you make some changes in what you do with your money, and ultimately in how you relate to your money, you really can create financial security, now and for your future too.

"Let me introduce you to the Necessity Board," I continue. "You and I are going to transfer most of the expenses you recorded for our meeting today onto your Necessity Board. Just like the name implies, these are your committed expenses, the bills that must be paid, e.g. mortgage, electricity, your car payment, etc. On the other side of your Necessity Board is your Reward Board. You are unique, Francesca, in that most of my clients would be hard-pressed to transfer some expenses that they consider to be necessities onto the other side of their boards. For example, some might consider their daily cup of fresh brewed halfcaf, halfdecaf with vanilla soy milk to be a necessary purchase."

"Seriously?" asks Francesca.

"Yes, indeed! Yet when we work with their actual income, they come to see that their little daily cup of java is costing them upwards of $120.00 per month – over $1,500.00 each year. Imagine that!"

Francesca looks like I just asked her to eat an entire Death by Chocolate cake in one sitting. "Unthinkable!" she exclaims.

"For you, yes," I reply. "Maybe for some of my other clients as well. But I don't just work with the in-coming and out-going money pieces of your puzzle. As we discussed earlier, there's more to managing your money than the numbers on your budget sheet. My hope is that you and I can plan financially for a life that you can enjoy living."

Francesca becomes pensive, staring out my window with a faraway look in her eyes. I give her a minute and then I ask,

"What's going through your mind right now?"

She snaps back to the present moment with a heavy sigh. "There's something about that word *enjoy*… I just flashed back to when I was a little girl, maybe six years old. One of the neighborhoods in which we lived had a beautiful lake with one of those tire swings, you know?" I nod, picturing a car tire tied to a rope and hanging from a big tree branch at the edge of a lake. "We would take turns swinging on the tire then pushing someone else, my friends and I. It was so much fun… I loved swinging higher and higher and then pushing off the tire and flying into up in the air, then plunging down into the lake." Her tone has become wistful.

"That sounds so delightful."

"Yeah, it was…" she says. "But, you know, I was just a kid. We had time for fun back then."

"And now?"

The question hangs between us for about a minute. Finally Francesca looks into my eyes and says, "I don't really spend much time enjoying life anymore."

"I know," I say with heartfelt understanding.

"Life just got so heavy, so laden with responsibilities. Ever since I was a teenager I took care of my siblings and in many ways, my parents as well," she explains. "If I didn't do it, it didn't get done. And I became increasingly responsible for budgeting our family's money. So, I made everything black and white–allocating funds where we absolutely needed them, and restricting expenses everywhere else."

"Sounds like you essentially became the parental figure in your family," I comment. "That's remarkable, Francesca. But what a burden for someone so young to carry…" She nods, lost in thought.

"What if I told you that a scarcity mentality can actually restrict your income? What if I told you that I believe that enjoying life *is* a necessity?"

"I've never considered that."

"I believe that you once knew this to be true. When you were swinging from that tire and soaring into the sky, you knew that joy is as essential to life as oxygen! Francesca, you've been living your life in black and white for so long, you've forgotten how wonderful it is to sparkle in Technicolor."

"But I can't just romp around and play all day. I have a job, I have bills to pay," she argues.

Smiling, I continue. "You couldn't be irresponsible if your life depended on it! You're just not wired that way." She smiles in agreement. "What do you do for fun, Francesca?"

"Well, I like playing with Freddie and Freda," she replies.

"Your cats bring you a lot of joy. I can tell. OK, what else do you do for fun?"

She looks at me, bites her lower lip, and finally says, "I can't think of anything else…"

"Well, let me re-phrase my question. What would you *like* to do for fun? If you had all the time and money you ever needed… if your have-to's were handled, what would be some of your want-to's?" Sensing that she needs a little prodding, I add, "Ask your six-year-old self!"

And the flood gates open… "I'd like to rock climb and roller-blade and parachute from a plane and learn to play the drums and go to the movies and eat at the finest vegan restaurants and fly to Australia and swing from a flying trapeze!"

Francesca is practically breathless and I can't help but smile my face off. "You've transformed before my very eyes!" I tell her.

"Wow," she says. "That just burst out of me…"

"No wonder," I say. "I am wowed by your discipline, Francesca. But can we just agree that long-term deprivation just sucks the life right out of you?"

"Yes," she says laughing. "No doubt about it… You know, one of my favorite movies when I was a child was 'The Wizard of Oz.' And one of the parts I love the most is when Dorothy and Toto first land in Munchkin City, and everything goes from black and white to spectacular color. That scene just slays me every time.

 "Go figure," I say, nodding in agreement. "Now please stop me before I launch into my Munchkin imitation!"

She laughs again and says, "I wish you would!"

"Maybe next visit," I tell her, barely concealing a smile. "I do believe we've had a breakthrough today," I tell Francesca. "So let's transfer your new-found beliefs to your Necessity and Reward Boards, OK?"

"OK!" she says. For her, the necessities include join a gym with a rock wall, dinner with friends every other week … time for herself! Francesca's rewards run the gamut from getting a professional hair cut every other month to taking drum lessons and saving for a trip to Australia.

"What phenomenal work you did today," I say to Francesca. "I'm so proud of you! How do you feel?"

"I feel… lighter," she says. "I feel like something inside me just expanded."

"I'm not surprised. Whenever you let go of fear that restricts you, you welcome in trust, which fills you with faith. And then you remember."

"I remember?"

"You remember the Truth you knew so well when you were a child. There will *always* be enough." I put my hand on my heart and Francesca does the same. "Promise me that you will keep this knowing here in your heart," I say.

"I promise," she says. I give her a goodbye hug, and Francesca leaves my office with her hand on her heart and a spring in her step.

Note: Take a peek at Francesca's Necessity Board on the next page.

NECESSITY BOARD for Frugal Francesca
(Net Monthly Income = $5103)

Expenses:	$
Mortgage	$ 1400
Association Fees/Property Tax	$ 275
Utilities	$ 300
Internet, Cable, etc.	$ 100
Home maintenance and repairs	$ 200
Groceries	$ 500
Hobbies	$ 50
Car payment	$ 250
Fuel	$ 150
Car maintenance and repairs	$ 100
Medical Insurance payment	$ 250
Dental, Vision, and other expenses	$ 50
Prescriptions	$ 20
Other Education expenses	$ 100
Pet Food	$ 100
Veterinary visits	$ 30
Medications	$ 30
Cell Phone	$ 75
Professional services, ie, Legal, Accountant	$ 70
Total	**$ 4050**
Left Over for Rewards***Under the Mattress	**$ 1053**

Chapter 14

<u>Here Comes Generous Genevieve</u>

Genevieve enters my office holding her a notebook in one hand and a gift in the other. I usher her over to the conference table and before we even sit down, Genevieve is excitedly handing me the gift. "What's this?" I ask.

"Open it! Open it!" she gleefully replies. I unwrap the gift and open the box to find a beautiful porcelain figurine of a gray-and-white striped cat snuggling with her little fluff-ball of a kitten.

"Genevieve, this is just lovely… You shouldn't have."

Genevieve looks sincerely pleased as she says, "The last time we met we were talking about animals and you mentioned that you missed having a cat. I wouldn't dare presume to bring you a real live cat or kitten, so I got you the next best thing."

"You do this quite often, don't you – gift giving?"

"Yes," she says. "I really do love to give and when I saw that cat and her kitten, I just had to get it for you!"

"First of all," I respond, "your gift is so thoughtful. *You* are so thoughtful, and I thank you." Genevieve nods her head and humbly smiles. "Secondly," I continue, "when I said 'you shouldn't have' that was probably an accurate statement."

Looking puzzled, Genevieve says, "I'm not sure I know what you mean."

"I know," I reply. "But you will, soon."

I invite Genevieve to sit with me at the table, and she hands me her "homework" with some trepidation. "Tell me, Genevieve," I ask, "what are you worrying about right now?"

"Well, putting all of my expenses as well as my savings, or the lack thereof, on paper was more than a little eye-opening," she replies.

"In what ways?"

Genevieve shrugs. "I guess I never realized how much money I've spent without thinking, especially in certain categories."

"OK," I reply, "from now on we're working together to create a more secure financial future for you. What your paperwork tells me is where you've been. We're going to change the where-you're-going part for the better, OK?"

A wave of relief spreads across her face as she says, "OK. Sounds good."

I take a few minutes to review Genevieve's paperwork and I find that what I've suspected is spot on. "The good news is that you actually earn a decent living," I begin. "I know that your income is based on successfully managing an extremely busy veterinary clinic, and I can tell that you've worked hard, Genevieve. You're to be commended for that."

"Thank you," she says, blushing a bit. "What's the bad news?"

"Let's just say that your present financial puzzle is in need of some revamping," I respond. "I'd like to shine the light on those 'certain categories' you alluded to earlier."

I share with Genevieve that given her income, at this point in her life, I would have expected to see more money in her retirement account and much less credit card debt. "It's plain to see that you spend an inordinate amount of money on gifts and charities," I explain. "In fact, you spend over 15% of your monthly income in this particular category."

"I know, I know," she says. "Everyone tells me that I give too much. But giving feels so right to me!"

"Genevieve, you have such a big heart and I actually want you to be able to continue to give."

"You do?" she exclaims. "That's great! You get me…"

"I do, Genevieve, but I want you to know that you are stopping short of getting the point."

She looks perplexed. "How so?"

I explain to Genevieve that if she were to continue spend over 15% of her income on giving in one way or another, she will not only deplete her savings, she will also increase her credit card debt so much so that she could actually lose her home.

"Genevieve, I want you to be able to give from an over-flow of abundance in your life," I say. "You've been giving from under-flow, and it's depleting you in every conceivable way." I know I just struck a chord, and I can see that Genevieve is fighting tears.

"I don't know any other way of being." Her voice quivers. "I've always been like this."

"I want to help you get to the root cause so you can make a lasting and positive change in your behavior, and ultimately, in your financial future," I explain. "Let's say that you have a gorgeous flower garden. You've been lovingly tending to it, but you notice a weed or two threatening the survival of some of your favorite flowers. What would happen if you just snip the weeds and toss them away?"

"They'll just grow back," she replies. "You've got to pull them out by the roots to get rid of them."

"Yes," I say, "very true. So if I were to ask you to just cut back on giving and put the money you'd save into your 401K, you might do this for a little while. But after a few months, or more likely a few weeks, you'd find yourself UPS-ing a gift to your friend in Arizona, or buying a cheer-you-up present for your sister, or calling in a donation for 'Save the Emus.' Am I right?"

Genevieve laughs. "Eeesh… you've really got my number!"

I ask her if she'd like to share a little about her upbringing and her background so that I can better understand what is motivating her to give and give at her expense. She describes her parents as "generous beyond measure." They donated and collected money for many a charity. They took people in need into their already filled-to-capacity home. And although they worked hard and struggled financially, they had an over-abundance of love for their children. Genevieve remembered a time when she was four or five years old when she gave away her favorite stuffed animals to her friend who had broken her arm. She recalled sharing her lunch with students in grade school when they had none. Afterward, her belly was hungry, but her heart was full.

Throughout her life, Genevieve gave her time, her energy, her compassion, and her money to friends, family, even new acquaintances. She couldn't bear to see anyone (human or animal) suffering in any way. Time and time again, without a single thought for her own well-being, Genevieve gave of herself. Opportunistic people invariably took advantage of her generous nature, but that didn't stop Genevieve from giving, giving, and giving some more.

"How do you feel about being on the receiving end of the equation?" I ask.

She visibly shudders. "That's very uncomfortable for me." Understatement of the century….

"Why do you resist receiving?" I ask. "Don't you deserve to receive love and joy and gifts and money just like everyone else?"

Genevieve is quiet for several moments. Then she replies, "I feel like I always have to work hard and give so much to earn love and joy and gifts and money." And there it is–the underlying belief that is dictating her over-giving behavior.

"Genevieve, what if you deserve all of this and more just because you were born--just because you exist?" I ask. "Leaving yourself out of the giving and receiving equation has worked against you for far too long," I continue. "In fact, giving to yourself first is *not* selfish–for you, it is survival. My goal in working with you to help you better manage your money is for you to commit to giving more to yourself and saving more for your future. Instead of depleting all of your resources like you've been doing, by adding *yourself* into your financial equation, you will ultimately be able to give more to the causes you support in the long run. Remember when we discussed your dreams for your future? You said that you wanted to be able have more than enough money to give generously to your favorite animal charities and to take care of the ones you love. If you continue to work with me and follow my recommendations, you'll have a much better chance of being able to give, give, and give to your heart's content!"

Genevieve's practically bouncing in her chair as she says, "I'm with you! I get it! Wow…"

We begin to put a plan into place, and I introduce Genevieve to the Necessity Board. I recommend adding a "Give to Myself" category. We agree to discuss increasing her monthly contribution to her retirement account. When I suggest removing some of her charities, I get a little push-back. "Stay with me," I reassure her, "you can add them back. I promise."

Then I explain that once we see that she can live within her means and save enough money each month for her future, we can flip the board over and factor in her rewards. Immediately, Genevieve adds back her various charities.

"Promise me that you will only make these donations from money you have left over after you've paid your bills and contributed to your 401K and savings account each month," I request.

"I promise," she replies.

"I know it will be a challenge, but if you stop watching Animal Planet and opening mail from all of those foundations for children for a little while, it may make it easier for you," I suggest.

"Good idea," she agrees, nodding her head. "Remove temptation – like going on a temporary donation diet. Oy, I'll do my best!"

"That's all I ask, Genevieve," I respond. "Your new mantra can be 'Save more now, give more later.'" She nods, grinning, and with the classic 'I could have had a V-8' gesture, lightly smacks herself on the head.

We make another appointment and Genevieve gathers up all of her belongings. I thank her again for the feline figurine, give her a big hug and say, "As one of my favorite inspirational authors, Catherine Ponder, says, 'To thine own Self be generous!' I'm so happy to see you heading toward a financially secure future, Genevieve."

"Me too," she says. "And thanks for reminding me that I deserve it." You most definitely do, Genevieve... you most definitely do.

Note: On the next page see how generous Genevieve is by reviewing her Necessity Board

NECESSITY BOARD for Generous Genevieve
Net Monthly Income = $5103

Expenses:	$
Rent	$ 1300
Utilities	$ 300
Internet, Cable, etc.	$ 195
Groceries	$ 500
Dining	$ 300
Car payment	$ 300
Fuel	$ 200
Car maintenance and repairs	$ 100
Medical Insurance payment	$ 250
Dental, vision and other expenses	$ 30
Prescriptions	$ 60
Pet Food	$ 220
Veterinary visits	$ 80
Medications	$ 70
Cell Phone	$ 125
Charitable Donations	$ 500
Professional services, ie, Legal, Accountant	$ 70
Gifts	$ 564
Total	**$ 5164**
Left Over for rewards ***oops	**$ - 61**

Chapter 15

<u>The Return of Perfectionist Penelope</u>

I've been looking forward to Penelope's second appointment with me because I just knew she was going to wow me with the way she prepared her "homework." She enters my office wearing a perfectly put-together professional outfit, briefcase in one hand as she shakes my hand firmly with the other. I show her to my conference table and Penelope proceeds to extract a notebook with several color-coded sections. "Very impressive," I comment.

"Thanks," she replies. "But I could have done a better job if I'd had more time."

As she sits down I notice that Penelope's rubbing her temples, looking more than a little tense. So I ask, "Was there something about gathering up your financial information that was stressful, or are you just having a rough day?"

"Yes and yes," she responds. "I'm a single mom and I never feel like there's enough time to do justice to managing our finances on top of everything else I take care of for my children, for my job…" I nod and Penelope continues. "Last night I was putting the finishing touches on my financial documents for our appointment, helping my son with his algebra homework, hemming my daughter's cheerleading skirt, and preparing a business plan for my boss while doing several loads of laundry. Is it any wonder that my whites are now pinkish?" She looks downright dejected.

"First of all," I begin, "I'm glad you're sharing all of this with me. The more I learn about you and your life, the more I can help you put the pieces of your puzzle together, creating the picture of the life you and your family deserve to live. Secondly, I really relate with your situation because I was essentially a single mom as well. The stress of trying to be everything to everybody can be so overwhelming, particularly when you live your life with such high standards."

"Very true," says Penelope. "I tend to be a little hard on myself."

Smiling, I say, "Ya think?" Finally, I get an answering smile from Penelope.

"When we first met, you told me how much you want long-term financial security for you and your children. Remember?" Penelope nods. "May I propose a challenge?"

"Sure," she replies.

"For every stress-inducing and self-critical thought you have, I want you to make three positive statements about your life and yourself." Penelope looks at me as if I just asked her to wear white after Labor Day. "With all of the responsibilities you're juggling–both personally and professionally--I happen to believe that you cannot afford the luxury of a negative thought. Don't you want to put all the odds in your favor?"

"Well, of course."

"Every time you think a critical, judgmental thought, you are literally weakening yourself."

"How so?"

"Stand up," I say, "and I will show you.

—

"While I'm no physics professor, it is widely known that everything is energy – including and especially your thoughts. I'd like to demonstrate how what you think affects how you feel. Are you OK with this?"

"Yes, I am. In fact I'm very interested," she says.

"OK," I say, "You're right-handed, correct?" She nods, and we continue. "Then hold your right arm straight out in front of you at shoulder level," I instruct. "Now resist upward as I try to push your arm downward." Penelope does so and her arm holds strong. "Great! Now I'm going to ask you to think about how much you love your children." A warm smile spreads across her face and try as I might, I cannot push her arm down. "Now, Penelope, think about everything that's stressing you out–the pressures of your job, juggling all of your kids' activities, single-handedly managing your household…" I easily push her arm down. "OK, c'mon. Really resist me now!" Penelope regroups and holds her arm out as stiff and strong as she possibly can while continuing to think about all of the stressors in her life and down goes her arm, with barely any effort on my part.

"Whoa…" she says, "that's more than a little disconcerting."

"Yes, it is," I agree. "Now think about all of the ways in which you're critical of yourself – from your physical appearance"--I push a little and her arm goes down--"to your job performance"--down it goes once again--"to your time management while trying to be everything to everybody." Her arm goes down and stays down on that one.

I give Penelope a minute to process this exercise. "I can hear the wheels turning in that busy mind of yours," I finally say.

She turns and looks at me, somewhat dazed. "No wonder I'm so exhausted all the time. I didn't realize how much my own thoughts were working against me."

"Are you ready for the good news?" I ask. She nods vigorously. "All right, now hold your arm up in front of you once more." Penelope complies. "Think about giving birth to your two little miracles." She closes her eyes and smiles as I push and push but cannot get her arm to budge an inch. "Hmmmmm…" I comment. "Remember a time when you were really proud of yourself." Shoulders back, head held high, Penelope easily resists my efforts to push her arm down.

"Will ya look at that!" I exclaim. "Now," I request, "please repeat after me: I have more than enough time for everything I wish to accomplish… I am perfect just as I am… I am a wonderful, loving mother." Penelope repeats all of these statements, one by one. I could stand on her arm and jump up and down, but there is no way that stronger-than-strong arm of hers is going anywhere but up. "You see," I explain, "the more life-affirming thoughts you think, the more you'll actually enjoy your life!"

"I get it," she says, "I really get it, and not just intellectually. Wow…"

"I know," I reply. "There's nothing like physically experiencing something to validate the truth, is there?"

"Nope," says Penelope. "Now I just have to rise to your challenge and remember to nip those negative thoughts in the bud."

"You'll get better at it over time--it just takes some practice. I speak from experience," I tell her. "Wink, wink."

"I never would have expected this to be part of my financial planning with you," says Penelope. "But I'm so glad you took the time to teach me."

"I'm just reminding you of what you already know, but sometimes forget," I reply. "We all forget from time to time. Why are we here if not to help one another? Now don't make me start singing, 'People who need people…'" I tell her.

Penelope laughs, "I won't! I'm with you, it makes undeniable sense. "

I review Penelope's financial information and turn to her. "This really is so impressive, Penelope," I say. "Your records are impeccable."

"Well," she demurs, "I should have organized the receipts in better chronological order…"

"By the way," I interject, "you might want to consider how compliment-deflecting affects you…"

"Eeesh! You're right," she agrees. "I deflect compliments on a regular basis."

"I bet you do," I reply. "Doesn't exactly strengthen you, does it?"

"No," she says. "It does not."

And how do you think it affects the giver of the compliment?" "It probably doesn't strengthen them either," replies Penelope.

"Maybe," I say, "just maybe, receiving more compliments will lead to receiving more abundance, in every sense of the word."

It's time to introduce Penelope to the concept of the Necessity/Reward Board. We begin by listing the obvious necessary monthly expenses: mortgage payment, groceries, utilities, car payment, college fund, etc. She's pleased to see that her calculations were correct and that she will have a fair amount of money left after paying for her monthly necessities.

"Great! I can put even more money toward my kids' college funds," says Penelope.

She is just about to turn over to the Reward side of the board when I say, "But we're not done on this side of the board yet." She looks at me with a mixture of confusion and worry. "I'd like you to add a few more necessary categories."

"What did I miss?"

"YOU--you missed taking care of *you*," I reply. "So I'd like you to begin by including a gym membership."

"But, but, but…" she stammers.

"No but's on this one, my friend. I remember you telling me how burned out rather than pumped up you feel after each power walk. A little social interaction combined with fitness-inducing me-time is long over due, my friend. Unless, of course, you believe that your sanity is not a necessity…" I respond.

"I see your point," she concedes. "OK, we'll add a monthly gym membership fee as a necessity. But what else would I have to add?"

"How about some help," I reply. "You know, most financial advisors would not say to their clients, 'I think you should spend more money on this or that.' I certainly do not do so with most of my clients. Everyone is unique and I want you to know that what I am suggesting is really about investing in yourself. That said, I recommend that you hire someone to help clean your home–even once a month. Cleaning your home is very time consuming for you, is it not?"

"It is…" says Penelope.

"You have more than enough room in your budget and it will free up more time for YOU!"

She closes her eyes while pondering my suggestion. "Won't this take away from saving for my children's college fund?"

"Penelope," I reply, "you really can afford $100/month and even more. And you desperately need some time to unwind. "Speaking of unwinding, I have one more recommendation that I hope you will consider: a massage," I say. Penelope looks stunned and appalled… she's rendered speechless. I might as well have told her to go slap her neighbor with a dead fish! "I expected this reaction and this is only a suggestion," I tell her. "Penelope, you and I discussed your goals and dreams when we last met. It's crystal clear to me that your children are your number one priority."

"Yes, they are," she agrees.

"You are the most important person in their world. They need to know that you're not going to bonk out on them from overworking and under-resting. I'm sure it's not a news flash when I tell you that you are seriously in need of some R & R, as in relaxation and rejuvenation. You push, push, push through your days, accomplishing more than 10 people ever could.

But you have no down-time whatsoever. I wish I could persuade you to have a spa day, but I know better than to push your envelope too far too soon."

"But I could never even think of something so frivolous when my kids need me and there's always so much to be done," she argues.

I look at her through eyes of compassion and say, "This is something I had to learn too, Penelope. I was whirl winding from one responsibility to another for years, just like you. One day I realized that I was just so exhausted from being on constant adrenaline overload, that I had reached a point of diminishing returns. It was taking me twice as long to accomplish half as much because I was running on fumes.

You know of what I speak, don't you?"

"Yes," she nods wearily, "I do."

"Would you consider getting a massage maybe just once every season?"

Penelope blows out a long breath and finally says, "All right. But just once every three months- not more often than that."

"It's a deal," I agree. And we shake on it.

As I expect, she fills the Reward side of her board with gifts and activities for her children. I request that she describe one of her very own, just-for-Penelope dreams to me when she returns for her next appointment. She agrees so I figure I'll stop while I'm ahead. "This has been unexpectedly illuminating," she says as we complete our second visit.

—

"It's going to be a pleasure working with you. You're an exceptional woman, Penelope," I say.

She opens her mouth, just about to deflect the compliment when she catches herself, grins and replies, "Thank you."

"You're a quick learner," I say as I give her a congratulatory hug. "May the Force be with you!" I declare, eliciting one final smile from Penelope. As she walks away I can swear I hear her repeating, "I have more than enough time for everything I wish to accomplish… I am perfect just as I am… I am a wonderful, loving mother..."

Note: Look at Penelope's Necessity Board on the next page….is it perfect?

NECESSITY BOARD for Perfectionist Penelope
Net Monthly Income = $5103

Expenses:	$
Mortgage	$ 1600
Association Fees	$ 250
Utilities	$ 300
Internet, Cable, etc.	$ 195
Phone	$ 35
Home maintenance and repairs	$ 200
Groceries	$ 800
Car payment	$ 150
Fuel	$ 200
Car maintenance and repairs	$ 100
School costs	$ 200
Kids' Activities and lessons	$ 300
Medical Insurance payment	$ 250
Dental, Vision and other expenses	$ 30
Prescriptions	$ 60
Cell Phone	$ 125
Education Savings	$ 25
Professional services, ie, Legal, Accountant	$ 70
Clothing	$ 200
Total	**$ 5090**
Left Over for rewards ***Perfect	**$ 13**

Chapter 16

<u>Time to Meet Savvy Sally</u>

If we were to combine the finest attributes from all four Money Mood characters and pour them into one woman, she would be one Savvy Sally! She would have a childlike sense of fun and carpe-diem spontaneity, just like Danielle. She would be prodigiously prudent and highly disciplined, just like Francesca. She would be oh so magnanimous and intensely compassionate, just like Genevieve. And our Savvy Sally would also have impeccably high standards and remarkable tenacity, just like Penelope. Here's a day in the life…

Savvy Sally sits back in her comfortable office chair, hands folded behind her head and a satisfied smile on her face. She swirls around to look out her floor-to-ceiling window at the gorgeous view of blue sky and majestic mountains. It inspires her every time, never fails. Sally takes a deep breath and closes her eyes as she reviews her productive, instructive day. She loves it when all of the necessary pieces of her daily puzzle fall right into place. Sally has learned to train her mind to expect to succeed, so she usually does. But this was not always the case.

She's traveled a long way on this journey of hers. Sally used to feast on fear in a variety of ways. She would begin her day with a bowl full of self-doubt. For lunch she would have either the poor-me soup or maybe the self-deprivation salad. She would snack on low-self-esteem chips or nibble on never-good-enough nutrition bars throughout the day. For dinner Sally would usually microwave some instant-gratification mac-n-cheese followed by some procrastination pudding. But at the end of the day all of these foods of fear never nourished Sally. So her belly was full, but her soul was starving.

She finally realized that the thoughts and feelings she was constantly feeding her mind could never sustain her–not if she wanted to live the life of her dreams. So little by little she began to feed herself thoughts of self-worth, self-love, and self-confidence. Over time she let go of her addiction to struggle and began to crave joy and self-expression. Sally gave herself permission to ingest passion and enjoy life. So now those old voices of doubt no longer out-shout her inner *knowing*. Sally knows beyond a shadow of a doubt that she deserves to be prosperous in every conceivable way. She is earning her living doing what she was born to do, a.k.a. right livelihood. Most importantly, Sally knows beyond a shadow of a doubt that she is having a massively positive influence on whoever walks through that door and into her office.

Sally started her day with her usual peace-of-mind-inducing meditation. She did not make time to give herself this gift yesterday and she was definitely not at her best. Feeling centered is an absolute must, especially given her inclination to take on too much too often. Without this crucial piece of her daily puzzle, she feels off her game and out of touch with her intuition. This does not a Savvy Sally make, so this morning she meditated her way back into the "peace and bliss zone" as she connected with her Higher Self. Waking up early enough to meditate and exercise takes discipline, and Sally has never run low on that. In fact, she has to keep an eye on this potentially rigid tendency of hers as she's been known to discipline her way straight to Dulls-ville. So, she has learned to balance out her have-to's with rewards in the form of want-to's. Once she re-fuels her emotional Self with heaping spoonfuls of vitality, the spring is back in her step in no time–every time!

On her way out the door she grabs her fruit smoothie and a bottle of water, and drives to her appointment with her personal trainer, Energetic Emmaline. Sally has recognized the folly in trying to do absolutely everything on her own, so she gives herself the gift of other people's expertise in ways that enhance her life. This was a long-overdue lesson, and is an on-going challenge because she is one self-sufficient woman. But she's finally realized that it's tough to be an expert in every field, so hiring Emma was a step in a healthier direction. Emma bounds over to Sally and greets her with a slightly devilish glint in her eyes. Sally wonders what Emma has in mind for today's training session so she asks, "So what are you planning to put me and my body through this morning?"

Emma smiles and replies, "Well, my dear Sally, whatever we do in this morning's workout is actually up to you!"

"Me?" she responds with her voice climbing up at least one octave.

"Yes, *you!*" says Emma. "I'd like to speak with your inner six-year-old and ask her what athletic gift she wants to give her body this morning."

As she closes her eyes, Sally finds herself smiling and actually bouncing up and down ever so slightly and she blurts out, "Climbing! I want to go climbing up a great big rock!"

"Then a-climbing we will go!" says Emma. "Follow me," she tells Sally as they head to the rock wall. After a phenomenally fun and exceptionally exhilarating workout, Sally drives home and jumps in the shower feeling invigorated, energized, and excited to begin her day.

Sally has been told more and more often that she dresses for success. While she does wear clothes that reflect her inner state of confidence, elegance, and prosperity, Sally now knows that the respect she commands follows her wherever she goes because of who she has become rather than what outfit she chose to wear that morning. She used to wear designer this and haute couture that. But when she didn't feel comfortable in her own skin, all the Christian Louboutin shoes and Gucci purses in the world couldn't make up for her lack of self-possession. And besides, when you've got that inner glowing going on, you radiate no matter what you wear.

Her booming Eco-Friendly Interior Design business is the result of years of hard work and dedication as well as the often intangible but ever-present energy she radiates. Sally used to experience a lot of insecurity, fearing that failure was lurking around every corner. Pushing to be perpetually perfect was actually the perfect formula for what Sally used to call "failure" and now calls "experience." When her adrenal glands finally waved the white flag, she was forced to surrender. Then the realizations flowed! Only when she took care of herself could she take care of others. Only when she began to trust her instincts could she step out of the stream of struggle and tap into the flow of blessings. And only when she learned to operate from that high-vibing inspired place did Sally experience the synchronistic events that she has come to expect on a daily basis.

As Sally gets ready to leave for lunch with a friend, her administrative assistant reminds her that they need to find one more "substantial" client to reach their monthly goal. Sally ponders this as she drives to the restaurant, refusing to let her old pal, Panic, steer her life. As she waits for her friend to arrive, Sally strikes up a conversation with an amiable couple who happened to sit in the booth next to hers. They tell her that they have just retired and relocated to her town. Sally listens and learns that they have been talking about re-designing their home, as they recently inherited a substantial sum of money. Hmmm… Apparently, they want to work with someone can who help them go green–to create an environment of earthy elegance in their new home. Sally smiles and explains that this is her passion and her area of expertise. She hands them her business card as they make an appointment to meet with her in the coming week. On her way back to the office, Sally finds herself happily humming and thinking, "Synchronicity strikes again!"

After lunch Sally finalizes plans on an environmentally friendly elementary school. So very rewarding, in more ways than she could have imagined. Her office manager, Meticulous Marissa, stops in to let Sally know that she was just awarded a project that is near and dear to her heart: an eco-friendly women's shelter. Sally has given many a seminar at that shelter and was moved to tears when the board voted to implement an interior design scholarship program for these most deserving women. Sally and Marissa have their weekly meeting, and it looks like her second office should be up and running within a month! It's *all* good, and it's also a lot more work. Uh oh, did she just take on too much, again?

Before the waves of overwhelm begin to flow, she takes a deep breath. Sally realizes that she is going to need some expert advice as she dives into these projects, in addition to her second office, not to mention her other day-to-day responsibilities. As she has been known to over-stretch herself a time or ten, getting better at delegating is a must now more than ever. Aware of her perfectionist tendencies, Sally of the High Standards has learned not to berate herself and does her best instead to learn from experience. She reminds herself that she is still part of the human race, and that we humans are allowed to be less than perfect now and again. This is a new phase of life, and she's heading into un-chartered waters. Sally picks up the phone and dials her financial advisor. It's time to work smarter, not harder. It's time ask for help in learning how her money can exponentially grow!

Chapter 17

<u>My Wishes for You</u>

My wish for you is that you've experienced many a miracle as you've read this book. I hope you have shifted your perception of who you are and how you relate to money. You may have previously defined yourself by your perceived limitations--but you know better, now.

You might have thought that you were destined to impetuously spend money and live under the burden of heavy debt. Now you know that the instant gratification of impulse buying is far outweighed by the sense of fulfillment you achieve by saving for a prosperous-in-every-way future. You may have believed that you had to maintain rigid control over your money and sacrifice joy for some semblance of security. Now you realize that by letting go of these fearful restrictions, you welcome in more faith, freedom, and abundance than you've ever imagined.

Maybe you were constantly compelled to give and give at your expense, sacrificing your own financial security in the name of altruism. Now it's clear that by giving to yourself first and by graciously receiving from others, you are actually able to contribute much more in the long run.

You could have been living under the constant pressure of the never-good-enough, feeling drained and frustrated too much of the time. Now you're convinced that by saying "Adios!" to those repetitive hyper-critical voices in your head, and replacing them with life-affirming thoughts and actions, you are welcoming in a wealth of health, joy, and prosperity.

Now you know how to maximize each and every one of your attributes. You have also become aware of certain tendencies that once dictated your less-than-desirable money modus operandi. You are also cognizant and capable of making these tendencies actually work in your financial favor. In other words, you are making the most of your Money Mood!

My wish for you is that you now know, beyond a shadow of a doubt that going for your dreams is anything but selfish. If you really want to breathe easier about taking better care of yourself and the ones you love, fulfilling your dreams is definitely the ultimate oxygen mask.

You realize that the dream seeds that were planted in you can only flourish in your unique and glorious garden. You are crystal clear not only about what lights you up, but also about just how imperative it is for you to keep that inner glowin' goin' on!

Bringing your dreams to fruition is the ideal incentive for adhering to the improvements you've made in your Money Mood. By participating full-on in the process of growing your dreams, you've discovered the consummate impetus for creating financial security.

My wish for you is that you appreciate the value of your Necessity Board. Being financially responsible for life's necessities promotes a good night's sleep and plenty of peace of mind, both of which are absolutely priceless. And the rewards on the flip side of that board are mighty enjoyable too!

So when you're watching QVC and that old instant gratification voice urges you to buy now and screw the consequences, your wiser, more mature voice can now speak up and remind you that delaying gratification now leads to more rewards later. If your former scarcity mentality tempts you hide a couple hundred bucks in a baggie under the frozen peas in the freezer, call upon your trusting voice to guide you to invest that money, and maybe take in a movie. When you're reading a fabulous book and you feel the urge to buy a copy for everyone you know and love, take a deep breath before visiting amazon.com. Regroup and remember that recommending this book to your friends and family is more than enough. If they are interested, they can buy it for themselves, and you can put the money you would have spent on all of those gifts into taking care of *yourself* and your financial future. Your inner task-master may occasionally threaten to overtake you with one more get-this-done-perfectly-now assignment at 11:00p.m. when you're already too pooped to pop. Instead of letting that old drill sergeant accuse you of being a slouch, you now can channel the voice of self-care and say "Thanks for sharing" as you head to your bed for a rejuvenating night's sleep.

My wish for you is to be proud of the moment-to-moment awareness you're cultivating in replacing those old repetitive habits with your prosperity-conscious thoughts and behaviors. Remember that this is a one-step-at-a-time journey. And you've already taken the most important step by heading in the financially healthier and wealthier direction. While you may have previously believed that you were just destined to repeat those self-defeating, life-diminishing behaviors, you now know that all it takes is one shift in perception to change your life for the better. Over time, the day-to-day decisions you make with your new and improved life-affirming state of mind accumulate. Before you know it, you will have changed the trajectory of your life and literally altered your destiny.

Michelangelo once explained that he believed the statue of David already existed within that block of stone. It was his job to chip away the excess marble in order to reveal God's masterpiece.

My wish for you is knowing that your own version of Savvy Sally lives in you. Every time you chip away one of your old limiting beliefs, you will reveal more of the masterpiece of you.

My grandest wish for you is for your life to be filled with miracles. And if all of my heartfelt wishes for you come true, then all of your wishes will come true, too...

APPENDIX

Answer Key

Determining Your Money Mood

Now that you've taken the quiz (hope you had a laugh or two), it's time to "score" it.

Examine each answer carefully. You will quickly notice each answer correlates to one of the four Money Mood personalities (identified below). To calculate your Money Mood write down the personality you chose for each question (e.g. if you chose "C" for question 1, you'd write down Generous Genevieve). Once you've finished this for each of the 8 questions, total the number of each of the Money Mood personalities. Your Money Mood will be the personality you selected most often. If you have an equal number of selections, you may be a hybrid, as we mentioned earlier.

F = Frugal Francesca   D = Debtor Danielle   G = Generous Genevieve   P = Perfectionist Penelope

Quiz Answer Key

1 – When I think about saving money for my future:

A=(D);   B=(F);   C=(G);   D=(P);

2 – As far as following a budget goes:

A=(D);   B=(F);   C=(P);   D=(G);

3 – The way I feel about credit cards is:

A=(F);   B=(P);   C=(G);   D=(D);

4 – I would borrow money:

A=(P);   B=(G);   C=(D);   D=(F);

5 – My favorite Uncle Fred unexpectedly left me $75,000 in his will. I am inclined to:

A=(P);   B=(D);   C=(F);   D=(G);

6 – To me money means:

A=(F);   B=(G);   C=(D);   D=(P);

7 – If, God forbid, I had to deal with an emergency:

A=(P);   B=(D);   C=(G);   D=(F);

8 – I'm in the mall and I see something I don't really need, but I REALLY want:

A=(G);   B=(D);   C=(F);   D=(P);

Character Summaries

Debtor Danielle --

ATTRIBUTES = Lives very much in the NOW; experiences a lot of fun and adventure living in this spontaneous, vivacious, carpe diem manner; believes that life is to be enjoyed!

CHALLENGES = Instant-gratification oriented: buy now and experience the euphoria, then pay later and experience the anxiety and the shame; impatient, impetuous and heavily in debt.

If your responses reflect Debtor Danielle's Money Mood, you possess an incredible passion for life! You hold the torch of fun and adventure for those of us who seriously need to lighten up! You often exhibit a childlike spontaneity, which is refreshing and much needed in our society. However, as a mature woman you realize that the instant gratification of impulse buying is often followed by delayed anxiety. And your lack of financial preparedness is keeping you up at night. Consequences, don't like 'em one bit, and yet they are a fact of life. But never fear, Danielle! You don't have to wear gray and restrain your joie de vivre! Let me show you how you can become just as "addicted" to saving money as you were to spending it!

Frugal Francesca –

ATTRIBUTES = Exceptionally efficient and thrifty with money; simple needs make her very low maintenance; makes well-thought-out buying decisions; highly disciplined human!

CHALLENGES = Stringently tight controls over her money and her life; often pays with cash only and does not build credit; rarely makes time to have fun and enjoy life.

If your dominant Money Mood is that of Frugal Francesca, you are to be commended! Your ability to exert rigorous control over your finances, as well as many other aspects of your life, is a rare and inspiring attribute. You know that you are not necessarily cheap, nor are you always rigid. In fact, your ability to discipline yourself is quite laudable, indeed! It's likely that you are often uptight about money and can sometimes limit your life by playing it too safe and secure. Living too small a life will never do for you, Francesca – especially when you've got such an expansive Spirit! Rather than putting all of your effort into trying to contain that kind of power, why not apply that exemplary discipline and thoughtful nature of yours to learning more about what money can do for you? Fun and freedom (on your terms) are yours to claim!

Generous Genevieve –

ATTRIBUTES = "Live to give" mentality; very magnanimous, compassionate nature; often involved in worthy causes; BIG heart!

CHALLENGES = Has trouble saying NO; takes care of others at her own expense; gives to everyone but herself and neglects her own financial future.

If your Money Mood answers add up to Generous Genevieve, you are one loving and lovable woman! If only others were 1/100 as altruistic as you… Your natural inclination is to give, give, and give some more. They broke the mold of compassion when they made you, Genevieve. But you were not born with a permanent defect in your instincts for self-preservation. You've acquired this proclivity for selflessness and by now you've realized that it doesn't always work in your favor. In fact, a lifetime of over-giving has left you feeling drained of energy and full of stress. Genevieve, you and that heart of yours are mighty powerful, so hold tight to your generosity! You need not, nor could you ever, morph into a selfish person. But you do need to fill your own cup before you can overflow enough to bestow your precious energy upon others. Together we can redirect all of that caretaking into taking care of you and your finances!

Perfectionist Penelope –

ATTRIBUTES = Excellent work ethic; high achiever in every aspect of her life; extremely focused and productive – can do the job of ten humans!

CHALLENGES = Never satisfied and often frustrated; has trouble relaxing; hyper-critical of herself, and sometimes others; stressed out much of the time.

If your Money Mood resonates with Perfectionist Penelope, you truly are extraordinary. You are a force of nature! Who gets more done in one day than you? No one, that's who! Your standards of excellence soar beyond the stratosphere and when you set a goal for yourself, you don't just achieve it, you surpass it! You know how to be productive every moment of the day like nobody's business. But you're never really satisfied, are you? You push and push your envelope relentlessly, always feeling pulled in a thousand directions. How long before you reach a point of diminishing returns? Your adrenal glands are waving the white flag and your ATP is about to plotz! The more you deplete your physical and emotional energy, the further you seem to deplete your bank account. Maybe a new way of life will reveal a new Penelope to you… It's time to learn how to apply your remarkable tenacity to living a healthier, wealthier life!

Necessity Board

Category	Expense	Amount
Home	Rent/Mortgage	
	Association Fees	
	Utilities	
	Internet, Phone, Cable, etc.	
	Maintenance and Repairs	
Food	Groceries	
	Dining	
Trans-	Car Payment	
portation	Fuel	
	Maintenance and Repairs	
	Tolls, Parking, Public	
	Transportation, etc.	
Children	School Costs	
	Extracurricular Activities	
	Child Support	
	Alimony	
Medical	Insurance Payment	
	Office Visits, RXs, etc.	
	Alternative Treatment	
Pet	Food	
	Veterinary Visits, RXs, etc.	
Personal	Cell Phone	
	Beauty and Fitness	
	(Gym, Salon costs, etc.)	
	Professional Services	
	(Attorney, Accountant, etc.)	
	Miscellaneous	
	(Clothing, Household,	
	Gifts, Donations, Etc.)	

About the Author

Susan McEuen, CFP®, ChFC®, a successful financial advisor, was raised by a single mother of four who struggled financially throughout her entire life. She vowed to become an expert in this field and create her own financial abundance and independence. Her mission is to teach and inspire other women to do the same.

Owning a thriving financial planning practice for thirty plus years, Susan holds the professional designations of Certified Financial Planner™ and Chartered Financial Consultant™. She has received the President's Advisory Counsel Award and The Diamond Ring Hall of Fame Award (the top 1% of advisors within our franchise of 10,000 advisors).

To contact Susan for assistance please use the Contact Form available on the website.

www.MoneyMoodBook.com

www.ingramcontent.com/pod-product-compliance
Lightning Source LLC
Chambersburg PA
CBHW071005040426
42443CB00007B/678